Abraham Lincoln's Gettysburg Address

Abraham Lincoln's Gettysburg Address
Four Score and More

BARBARA SILBERDICK FEINBERG

Twenty-First Century Books
Brookfield, Connecticut

In memory of my beloved Yorkshire terrier, Katie
(December 17, 1984–September 1, 1998)

I would like to thank Virginia Koeth, formerly of Twenty-First
Century Books, for suggesting that I write about Lincoln and the
Gettysburg Address. Suzannah Schatt deserves praise for her efficiency
and effectiveness as my research assistant. After I spent hours brain-
storming and came up empty-handed, Gina Cane, a cherished friend,
came to my rescue and once more supplied me with a book title. I
very much appreciate her help. Most of all, I am grateful to my editor,
Dominic Barth, who skillfully turned my manuscript into a book and
proved to be a witty and delightful conversationalist.

Published by Twenty-First Century Books
A Division of The Millbrook Press, Inc.
2 Old New Milford Road, Brookfield, CT 06804
www.millbrookpress.com

Cataloging-in-Publication Data is on file at the Library of Congress.

Cover photographs courtesy of The Granger Collection, New York and Superstock

Photographs courtesy of The Granger Collection, New York: pp. 8, 18, 22, 25 (both), 26, 43 (top, bottom
right), 48, 54, 55, 67, 68; Library of Congress: pp. 15, 27, 34, 41; National Portrait Gallery, Smithsonian
Institution; Meserve Collection: pp. 30, 44 (right); National Archives: p. 44 (left); Adams County Historical
Society, Gettysburg, Pennsylvania: p. 46; © Corbis: p. 49; National Portrait Gallery, Smithsonian
Institution/Art Resource, NY: p. 64; © Glen Allison/Tony Stone Images: p. 70

∽ Contents ∽

Abraham Lincoln's Gettysburg Address

Abraham Lincoln in a photograph taken eleven
days before he gave the Gettysburg Address.

Washington, _____, 186

Four score and seven years ago our fathers brought

CHAPTER ONE

Four Score and More

Four score and seven years ago our fathers brought forth on this continent, a new nation, conceived in Liberty, and dedicated to the proposition that all men are created equal.

Now we are engaged in a great civil war, testing whether that nation or any nation so conceived and so dedicated can long endure. We are met on a great battle-field of that war. We have come to dedicate a portion of that field as a final resting place for those who here gave their lives that that nation might live. It is altogether fitting and proper that we should do this.

But in a larger sense we cannot dedicate, we cannot consecrate, we cannot hallow this ground. The brave men, living and dead, who struggled here have consecrated it far above our power to add or detract. The world will little note, nor long

rth, upon this continent, a new nation, conceived

a liberty, and dedicated to the proposition that

remember what we say here, but it can never forget what they did here. It is for us the living, rather, to be dedicated here to the unfinished work which they who fought here have thus far so nobly advanced. It is rather for us to be here dedicated to the great task remaining before us; that from these honored dead we take increased devotion to that cause for which they here gave the last full measure of devotion; that we here highly resolve that these dead shall not have died in vain; that this nation, under God, shall have a new birth of freedom; and that government of the people, by the people, and for the people shall not perish from the earth.

This is the official text of Abraham Lincoln's famous Gettysburg Address. Year after year, schoolchildren memorize these 272 words, but they are not completely identical to the ones Lincoln spoke on November 19, 1863, during the Civil War. The speech that students learn to recite is based on the last existing copy of the text in Lincoln's handwriting and contains some changes he made to improve its style. Historians still have not found the original draft of the speech that the president used at Gettysburg. Lacking audiotapes and similar technology, they must rely on other sources to reconstruct what Lincoln actually said. Historians study newspaper reports of the speech based on the shorthand notes of reporters who were there. Then they compare these with later versions that the president corrected, wrote out, and gave away.

Historians have tried to solve a number of other issues concerning the Gettysburg Address. One of the most perplexing

"all men are created equal"

Now we are engaged in a great civil war, test

problems is when the president wrote the speech. Eyewitness accounts are not entirely reliable. Some claim that he dashed it off at the last minute, while others insist that he prepared it in advance. These observers also supply differing interpretations of the president's reaction to his address. Was he proud of it, or did he think it was a failure? The memoirs of his friends and aides support both views. In the absence of opinion polls, the public's response is just as hard to determine. In addition, historians have disagreed about the purpose of the speech. A few have argued that it was a clever piece of propaganda intended to help Lincoln and the Republican party win the next election. Others have claimed that it was meant to heal the divided nation.

The content of the Gettysburg Address creates another set of problems for historians. For example, the president claimed that the American Republic was founded "four score and seven years ago" (1776), the year the Declaration of Independence was written, rather than three score and sixteen years ago (1787), the year the Constitution was completed. Why did he choose the earlier date?

Lincoln's attitude toward slavery and the rights of black people provokes controversy. Because his views evolved over time, they were not always clear or consistent. In the Gettysburg Address, Lincoln insisted that "all men are created equal." He certainly did not agree with Southerners who regarded their slaves as property. Yet he was not an abolitionist. While he reluctantly freed southern slaves, he did nothing about the slaves in the border states that sided with the North during the Civil War. So did he feel that black people were only entitled to basic, or natural, rights to be treated human beings, or was he offering them something more?

hether that nation, or any nation so conceived,

nd so dedicated, can long endure. We are met

Finally, historians must explain why the Gettysburg Address has become such an important part of the nation's heritage. Lincoln's speech took less than three minutes to deliver, and he was not the main speaker that day. Yet his words have inspired later presidents, poets, composers, and filmmakers. Why has the speech continued to appeal to generations of Americans?

To find the answers to these and other questions about the Gettysburg Address, historians must act like detectives. They will return to the scene of the events in dispute and try to reconstruct what may have happened. New information may be waiting to be discovered, or new interpretations may be found for what is already known. That is why history can be an exciting adventure for those who travel back in time.

on a great battle field of that war. We have come to dedicate a portion of it, as a final re

CHAPTER TWO

The Dedication Ceremony

By November 19, 1863, about 15,000 people had arrived in Gettysburg, Pennsylvania, a town of about 2,500 inhabitants. They had come to witness the dedication of a national cemetery to honor the Union soldiers slain in one of the bloodiest battles of the Civil War. Some estimates put the number of visitors as high as 30,000. A reporter for *The New York Times* wrote:

> *All the hotels as well as private houses were filled to overflowing last night. Every housekeeper in Gettysburg has opened a temporary hotel and extends unbounded hospitality to strangers—for a consideration. People from all parts of the country seem to have taken this opportunity to pay a visit . . . .*

On this cold, foggy morning, many of them as well as reporters waited to catch a glimpse of President Abraham Lincoln as he prepared to leave for the ceremonies. Earlier, he had toured the battlefield with Secretary of State William Seward.

The president appeared promptly at ten, wearing a black suit, a black silk top hat, and white gloves. Lincoln had just received a telegram from Secretary of War Edwin M. Stanton, telling him about the status of the Union campaign in Tennessee. Stanton also added, "Mrs. Lincoln reports your son's health as a great deal better and he will be out today." The president was relieved that Tad had recovered from a fever. Lincoln still wore a mourning band on his top hat in memory of his son Willie who had died in 1862.

The 6-foot, 4-inch (193-cm) president mounted a chestnut horse as he prepared to take part in the procession to the cemetery. After a considerable search, the parade organizers had found a horse large enough for him. The streets were too narrow for carriages to be used. A young lieutenant accompanying him wrote: "His towering figure surmounted by a high silk hat made the rest of us look small." As soon as Lincoln appeared on horseback, he was mobbed by people eager to shake his hand. He bent over to greet them while the parade marshals tried to break up the crowd and get the procession under way.

The fifteen-minute march wound its way through the main streets of Gettysburg, passing buildings and homes with flags at half staff. Despite the festive atmosphere, the townspeople had not forgotten why so many officials and soldiers were parading past them. Secretary Seward and Postmaster General Montgomery Blair rode to the right of the president, while Secretary of the Interior John P. Usher and Chief Marshal Ward H. Lamon rode to his left. Following them were presidential secretaries John Hay and John Nicolay and military officers leading regiments of cav-

larger sense, we can not dedicate—we can no consecrate—we can not hallow, this ground—

The parade to the cemetery, November 19, 1863

alry and infantry. John Russell Young, a correspondent for the *Philadelphia Press*, described the procession as "a ragged affair" that "added to the confusion, and not much to the dignity of the day." The participants arrived at the cemetery around eleven thirty.

A platform had been erected, overlooking the battlefield. Military troops formed a large square around the platform, surrounding some 15,000 to 20,000 people who were watching the ceremonies. Reporters sat on one side of the platform. Officials and dignitaries occupied the other, including the governors of Indiana, Maryland, New Jersey, New York, Pennsylvania, and Ohio as well as some members of Congress, foreign ministers, and Union Army generals. (Major General George G. Meade, in command of the army during the Battle of Gettysburg, had declined to come to the ceremonies because of the pressure of military duties.) The president sat between Secretary Seward and the seat reserved for Edward Everett, the featured speaker. The sixty-nine-year-old Everett was delayed, so military bands played until noon when he took his place beside Lincoln.

The Reverend Thomas H. Stockton, chaplain of the U. S. House of Representatives, opened the program with a prayer, asking God to bless the defenders of the Union. As he spoke, the sun came out, breaking up the fog that had made this cold autumn day even more somber. He praised the slain soldiers: "As the trees are not dead, though their foliage is gone, so our heroes are not dead, though their forms have fallen. In their proper personality they are with Thee. And the spirit of their example is here." A reporter for the *Cincinnati Daily Gazette* noted that President Lincoln was moved to tears by the prayer, and the *Philadelphia Press* correspondent wrote, "There was scarcely a dry eye in all that vast assemblage."

to add or detract. The world will little note, nor remember what we say here; while it can neve

Benjamin B. French, superintendent of buildings in Washington, D.C., took the podium and introduced Edward Everett, the main speaker of the day. Everett rose, bowed to the president, uttering the words, "Mr. President." The president replied, "Mr. Everett." Like the rest of the audience, Lincoln looked forward to Everett's melodious voice, flowery phrases, and dramatic gestures. The famous orator spoke from memory, deliberately ignoring the copy of his speech placed on a nearby table. He began:

> *Standing beneath this serene sky, overlooking these broad fields now reposing from the labors of the waning year, the mighty Alleghenies dimly towering before us, the graves of our brethren beneath our feet, it is with hesitation that I raise my poor voice to break the eloquent silence of God and Nature. But the duty to which you have called me must be performed . . . .*

His speech reviewed the manner in which the ancient Greeks honored their war dead; his audience expected such classical references. His voice was steady and deep, his stance erect; his white hair flipped back as he shook his head to make a point. After discussing the political and military events that led to the Battle of Gettysburg, he proceeded to describe the three-day conflict in great detail, mentioning the now famous sites on view behind the platform: "Seminary Ridge, the Peach Orchard, Cemetery, Culp, and Wolf Hill, Round Top, Little Round Top, humble names, henceforward dear and famous—no lapse of time, no distance of space, shall cause you to be forgotten." He pleased the local resi-

gets what they did here.
It is rather for us, the living, to stand here, we here be dedicate

This colored engraving of Edward Everett was based on a photograph by Mathew Brady, a photographer known today for his images of the Civil War.

ted to the great task remaining before us— that, from these honored dead we take indents by referring to familiar people and places: "General Reynolds directed his men to be moved over the fields from the Emmitsburg road in front of M'Millan's and Dr. Schmucker's, under cover of the Seminary Ridge." Everett frequently identified the individual units and their commanders in his account of the fighting. He also listed the names of the Union and Confederate generals who were wounded or killed.

Everett went on to ask who was responsible for all this bloodshed. He blamed the Confederacy and rebutted at great length the South's arguments for going to war. They claimed to be defending the rights reserved to the people and the states under the Tenth Amendment to the Constitution. They also insisted that the states retained their sovereign powers when they entered the Union. In a summation, he queried:

> [C]an it need a serious argument to prove that there can be no State right to enter into a new confederation reserved under a constitution which expressly prohibits a State to "enter any treaty, alliance, or confederation," or any "agreement or compact with another State or foreign power?"

Having condemned the Confederacy, he pleaded for reconciliation between the North and the South when the war was over. He ended his speech with the claim that in the history books, "there will be no brighter page than that which relates to the battles of Gettysburg." According to Nicolay, the audience cheered and applauded him. For almost two hours, he had held their attention with his "eloquent description," "polished diction," and "practised delivery."

creased devotion to that cause for which

they here, gave the last full measure of de-

Afterward, the Baltimore Glee Club sang a special hymn, with words written for the occasion by Benjamin French. Poets Henry Wadsworth Longfellow, William Cullen Bryant, John Greenleaf Whittier, and James Russell Lowell had declined an invitation to prepare the verses. Each one had claimed that he was too busy to do it.

Now it was time for the president to officially dedicate the cemetery. Following a brief introduction by Ward Lamon, Lincoln stood up, walked to the speaker's stand, and put on his steel-rimmed glasses. Pastor E. W. Andrews offered the following description: "President Lincoln was so put together physically that, to him, gracefulness of movement was an impossibility. But his awkwardness was lost sight of in the interest which the expression of his face and what he said awakened." In his hand, Lincoln held the two pages he had written and glanced at them while he spoke. His voice was steady but high-pitched. His Kentucky twang, with its "thar" instead of "there" and "forgit" instead of "forget," may have sounded strange and unpleasant to some of his listeners, but even those in the rear could easily hear him.

According to the shorthand notes taken by Associated Press reporter Joseph L. Gilbert, President Lincoln said:

> *Four score and seven years ago our fathers brought forth upon this continent a new nation, conceived in liberty, and dedicated to the proposition that all men are created equal. Now we are engaged in a great civil war, testing whether that nation or any nation so conceived and so dedicated can long endure. We are met on a great battle-field of that*

notion— that we here highly resolve these

dead shall not have died in vain, that

war. We are met to dedicate a portion of it as the final resting place of those who here gave their lives that that nation might live. It is altogether fitting and proper that we should do this. But in a larger sense we cannot dedicate, we cannot consecrate, we cannot hallow this ground. The brave men, living and dead, who struggled here, have consecrated it far above our power to add or detract. The world will little note nor long remember what we say here, but it can never forget what they did here. It is for us, the living, rather to be dedicated here to the unfinished work that they have thus far so nobly carried on. It is rather for us to be here dedicated to the great task remaining before us—that from these honored dead we take increased devotion to that cause for which they here gave the last full measure of devotion—that we here highly resolve that the dead shall not have died in vain; that the nation shall, under God, have a new birth of freedom; and that government of the people, by the people, and for the people, shall not perish from the earth.

Unlike Everett, Lincoln had not given the press an advance copy of his speech because he had not finished it before he arrived in Gettysburg. This is why Gilbert and other reporters had to make copies of the president's remarks while they listened to it.

Lincoln made some slight changes in the text as he spoke. Other changes, more familiar to modern readers, were made later when the speech was rewritten and copied by the president him-

This lithograph of Lincoln delivering his address wasn't
made until 1905. Apparently Lincoln's address was so short
that no photographer had made a presentable image
by the time he finished speaking.

the nation, shall have a new birth of free-

dom, and that government of the people by

self. His speech was far more abstract and general than Everett's. He was just as familiar with the details of the three-day battle, but he had only been invited to deliver a few remarks to dedicate the cemetery. Everett was the one chosen to give the main speech at the ceremony. In all, Lincoln's 272-word address took less than three minutes. John R. Young, a reporter for the *Philadelphia Press* wrote that the president's talk was over so quickly that a photographer failed in his attempt to record the moment for history.

After Lincoln returned to his seat, the assembled guests and spectators listened to a dirge, or funeral song, with words written by James G. Percival set to music by Alfred Delaney. Then Reverend H. L. Baugher, president of Pennsylvania College at Gettysburg, gave the benediction, bringing an end to the formal ceremonies. The crowds dispersed quietly, some returning to their homes or lodgings while others toured the battlefield.

The president, Mr. Everett, and other dignitaries had lunch at the home of David Wills, who had organized the dedication. Then they took part in an impromptu reception. For nearly an hour, they shook hands with hordes of visitors who wanted to meet them. At five o'clock, the president attended a meeting at the Presbyterian church, accompanied by John Burns, the only Gettysburg citizen who took up arms to assist the Union troops in defending his town. Burns was nearly seventy years old and a veteran of the War of 1812. On July 1, 1863, he fought beside troops from Pennsylvania and was wounded three times. Burns and President Lincoln listened to a speech by the incoming lieutenant governor of Ohio. At six-thirty, Lincoln and his guests left for Washington. During the six-hour train ride, the weary president stretched out on a seat in the drawing room car with a towel across his forehead. It had been a very long and sad day.

the people for the people, shall not per-
ish from the earth.

CHAPTER THREE

An Invitation to the President

From July 1 to July 3, 1863, the Confederate Army of Northern Virginia, commanded by General Robert E. Lee, and the Union Army of the Potomac, led by General George G. Meade, had fought one of the greatest battles of the Civil War at Gettysburg. Neither general expected to conduct a major military campaign in this small Pennsylvania town. However, when a Confederate unit accidentally ran into Union soldiers outside the town, a skirmish broke out. Commanders from each side rushed troops to the scene, and before long, they were engaged in a bitter and bloody conflict. Meade's army took a defensive position on Cemetery Ridge and managed to hold it against massive bombardment and against Pickett's charge, a dramatic but futile attack by 15,000 Confederate soldiers. General Meade never counterattacked, nor did he pursue the retreating Confederate forces when the battle was over.

Neither side had reason to be proud. Lee's army had advanced on Pennsylvania in the hope of convincing the war-weary North

Washington, _____, 186

Four score and seven years ago our fathers brought

General Robert E. Lee

Major General George G. Meade

that the South could not be subdued. His hopes were dashed after Gettysburg. Meade won the battle, but his delaying tactics failed to hasten the end of the war. In the course of the fighting, both armies had suffered heavy losses. According to writer Robert Leckie, the Army of the Potomac suffered 23,049 casualties; 3,155 men were dead, 14,529 wounded, and 5,365 missing, some of them captured. The Army of Northern Virginia had 27,788 casualties, with 3,903 killed in action, 18,735 wounded, and 5,150 missing or captured.

Burial of the dead and care for the wounded were left to the military and to local authorities. Union soldiers and their Confederate prisoners hastily dug graves at the battle site lest the remains of their fallen comrades spread disease throughout the town during the hot summer days. An enterprising businessman bought up land in the surrounding area. He realized that many

Confederate General R. S. Ewell's corps charge on Cemetery Gate at Gettysburg. Painted by Edwin Forbes based on sketches he made as an eyewitness to the battle.

grieving families would want to rebury their dead with suitable ceremonies, and the local cemetery would soon run out of space. The wounded outnumbered the citizens of Gettysburg and quickly filled the available hospitals. Pennsylvania Republican Governor Andrew G. Curtin arrived on the scene, with sorely needed medical supplies. He appointed David Wills as his local representative to see what more could be done.

"all men are created equal"

Now we are engaged in a great civil war, te...

Four dead soldiers in the Gettysburg woods near Little Round Top

hether that nation, or any nation so conceived, and so dedicated, can long endure. We are met

Wills was a thirty-two-year-old attorney and banker. He had studied law with Thaddeus Stevens, a famous resident of Gettysburg who went on to serve in Congress. Wills owned the largest home in the town square and took an active interest in local affairs. As the governor's representative, he made several trips to the battlefield. Wills realized that the fallen soldiers deserved a more appropriate resting place than a series of scattered, shallow, poorly marked graves. Also, the townspeople needed to be shielded from the unsanitary conditions and gruesome sights resulting from the hasty burials. Finally, Union families who had lost loved ones needed protection from unscrupulous attempts to sell them reburial sites at high prices. On July 24, Wills wrote to the governor, proposing to establish a national cemetery for the Union heroes of Gettysburg.

Once Governor Curtin approved the plan, he contacted the governors of the seventeen states whose soldiers had fought in the battle to ask for their cooperation. In the nineteenth century, states usually solved common problems by joint efforts rather than by requests for federal aid. The governors of Connecticut, Delaware, Illinois, Indiana, Maine, Maryland, Massachusetts, Michigan, Minnesota, New Hampshire, New Jersey, New York, Ohio, Pennsylvania, Rhode Island, West Virginia, and Wisconsin sent agents to Gettysburg to work with Wills. The federal government supplied caskets free of charge, but the rest of the expenses would be shared by the states. They decided to divide the costs according to the number of members the participating states sent to Congress. This seemed fairest since it was hard at this time to figure out how many soldiers each state had actually lost.

On August 17, Wills wrote to Curtin describing the property he had purchased for the cemetery:

on a great battle field of that war. We have come to dedicate a portion of it, as a final re-

The grounds embrace about seventeen acres on
Cemetery Hill, fronting on the Baltimore turnpike,
and extending to the Tarrytown road. . . . It is the
spot which should be specially consecrated to this
sacred purpose. It was here that such immense
quantities of our artillery were massed, and during
Thursday and Friday of the battle, from this most
important position the field, dealt out death and
destruction to the rebel army in every direction of
their advance.

The land cost $2,475.87. While Pennsylvania advanced the funds to buy the property, the other states paid their share and became joint owners. In his letter of August 21, Curtin expressed his satisfaction with the project. However, he cautioned Wills that the states might want to make some changes in his plans and that "it is my wish that you give to their views the most careful and respectful consideration."

The commission of state agents hired an architect, William Saunders, superintendent of grounds in the Department of Agriculture, to design the cemetery. He had studied landscaping in Scotland and was familiar with the "rural cemetery" movement. Starting in the 1830s, Americans had begun to move cemeteries outside of city churchyards and created parklike settings for the graves. This not only served to protect citizens from diseases but also to encourage them to better appreciate nature and the cycle of life and death.

For Gettysburg, Saunders planned to arrange the graves by state, in semicircular lots, divided into sections, with a 4-foot (1.2-

Governor Andrew Curtin

larger sense, we can not dedicate— we can not consecrate— we can not hallow, this ground—

meter) walk between each section. In this way, no state was given preference over another. However, some states, like New York and Pennsylvania, suffered greater losses than the other states, so more land was set aside to bury their dead. Saunders had to keep making adjustments in the plan once bodies were identified and sorted into their proper military units. Some graves were reserved for "unknown soldiers" whose names and ranks could not be determined. (After the war, many Confederate soldiers were reburied in the South.)

Wills felt that the grounds should be dedicated—even before the reburials took place. As was customary at the time, such ceremonies included inspiring speeches, with flowery phrases and dramatic gestures. The master of this type of oratory was Edward Everett, a distinguished American. During his lifetime, he had been a U. S. senator, the governor of Massachusetts, a member of the House of Representatives, President Millard Fillmore's secretary of state, professor of Greek at Harvard, president of Harvard University, and minister to Britain. Born in 1794, he was devoted to preserving the Union and the U. S. Constitution.

In his invitation to Everett on September 23, Wills scheduled the dedication for October 23. After describing the cemetery's design, he wrote to the orator that "the several states interested have united in the selection of you to deliver the oration on that solemn occasion." On September 26, Everett replied, asking for a change of date. "It is wholly out of my power to make the requisite preparation by the 23rd of October. I am under engagements which will occupy all my time from Monday next to the 12th of October . . . ." He went on to explain what his preparation involved and offered an alternative date:

The occasion is one of great importance, not to be dismissed with a few sentimental or patriotic commonplaces. It will demand as full a narrative of the events of the three important days as the limits of the hour will admit, and some appropriate discussion of the political character of the great struggle, of which the battle of Gettysburg is one of the most momentous incidents. As it will take me two days to reach Gettysburg, and it will be highly desirable that I should have at least one day to survey the battle-field, I cannot safely name an earlier time than the 19th of November.

Grateful that Everett would give the main speech, Wills readily agreed to change the date of the ceremony.

The commission sent out a printed circular inviting U. S. senators, representatives, the governors of Northern states, and members of the cabinet to Gettysburg. It is unclear whether a copy was sent directly to President Lincoln, but it did come to his attention. In any event, he notified the commission that he would attend the dedication. It was fitting that the head of the national government should attend the service.

Lincoln's response to the circular created a problem for the commission. They had to decide whether to ask him to give a speech. According to Clark E. Carr, the Illinois representative on the commission, "The question was raised as to his ability to speak upon such a grave and solemn occasion." Lincoln was known to include humor and folksy stories in his public speeches so that ordinary citizens would better understand the points he was making. Perhaps the commissioners feared that his remarks at Gettysburg would not be sufficiently dignified.

Lincoln, however, had a national reputation as a talented speaker. For example, in 1858, he accepted the Illinois Republicans' nomination for a seat in the U.S. Senate with a memorable speech that was featured in the newspapers of the day. He described his view of the tensions between the North and South with a biblical paraphrase "A house divided against itself cannot stand." The same year, his skillful arguments in debates with Democratic Senate candidate Stephen A. Douglas over the spread of slavery also received widespread coverage in the press. So perhaps the commissioners were needlessly worried about his ability to present a suitably somber address at Gettysburg.

Carr mentioned another concern, ". . . that, with his important duties and responsibilities, he could not possibly have the leisure to prepare an address." Other commissioners suggested that the president should be given the chance to decide these matters for himself, and that if he spoke, he would do what was "right and proper."

Wills, writing on behalf of Governor Curtin and the states, asked the president to dedicate the cemetery after Everett completed his oration. He requested that Lincoln prepare a solemn and dignified address. "It is the desire that after the oration, you, as Chief Executive of the nation, formally set apart these grounds to their sacred use by *a few appropriate remarks.*" [Italics added.] Perhaps Wills wanted to assure the commissioners that Lincoln's remarks would be dignified, not folksy, that the president would serve as a spokesman of national authority and not as a man of the people. Concluding his letter, he stated: "We hope you will be able to be present to perform this last solemn act to the soldier-

Gettysburg Nov. 2ᵈ 1863

To His Excellency,

    A. Lincoln,

    President of the United States,

       Sir,

          The several States

having soldiers in the Army of the

Potomac, who were killed at the

Battle of Gettysburg, or have since

died at the various hospitals which

were established in the vicinity,

have procured grounds on a

prominent part of the Battle Field

for a Cemetery, and are having

the dead removed to the

David Wills's invitation to Lincoln

ted to the great task remaining before u

that, from these honored dead we take

dead on this battle-field." Wills also wrote a separate note that read:

> *As the Hotels in our town will be crowded and in confusion at the time referred to in the enclosed invitation, I write to invite you to stop with me. I hope you will feel it your duty to lay aside pressing business for a day to come here to perform this last sad rite to our brave Soldier dead on the 19th instant.*
>
> *Governor Curtin and Hon. Edward Everett will be my guests at that time and if you come you will please join them at my house.*
>
> *You will confer a favor if you advise me early of your intentions.*

The decision to invite Lincoln to take part in the program seems to have been an afterthought. This was not, however, an attempt to deliberately insult the sixteenth president of the United States. The dedication ceremony was primarily a state-sponsored event, as was the purchase of the cemetery. In those days, most American citizens and their state governments did not expect the national government to become involved in their activities. Lincoln's participation in the program was not essential to its purpose—although his appearance, representing the national government, was welcome. Edward Everett was the main attraction. He would please the crowds with his gift for words. Lincoln knew this, too.

The two men respected each other despite differences in their backgrounds. Unlike Everett, Lincoln was a self-educated, backwoods lawyer. Between 1834 and 1842, he had served three terms in the Illinois state legislature and then one term in Congress in 1847. He had lost a bid for the Senate in 1858. At first, Everett had expressed doubts about the president's abilities. When Lincoln was elected in 1860, Everett had thought that he would be "wholly unequal to the crisis." However, he soon changed his mind, writing that the president was "one of the most laborious and indefatigable men in the country." He also appreciated Lincoln's "intellectual capacity." The president, in turn, admired the elderly orator. When Everett left on a trip to Europe in 1862, Lincoln gave him a letter of introduction, stating, "I am quite conscious that he could better introduce me than I him in Europe." Lincoln had a number of reasons for accepting Wills's invitation.

notion— that we here highly resolve that

dead shall not have died in vain, that

CHAPTER FOUR

The President's Response

Abraham Lincoln promptly accepted Wills's invitation to speak at the dedication ceremonies in Gettysburg. Unfortunately, later historians were unable to find his letter among Wills's papers or in the president's correspondence. Lincoln decided to go to Gettysburg because he wanted to honor the nation's fallen soldiers. The great number of lives lost in the three-day battle haunted him. As a concerned commander in chief, he had read the daily telegrams, military couriers' reports, and letters from the field with accounts of the devastating losses. As Wills wrote in his invitation, Lincoln's presence would

> *be a source of great gratification to the many*
> *widows and orphans that have been made almost*
> *friendless by the great battle here, to have you here*
> *personally; and it will kindle anew in the breasts of*
> *the comrades of these brave dead, who are now in*
> *the tented field or nobly meeting the foe in the*

the nation, shall have a new birth of free-
dom, and that government of the people by

front, a confidence that they who sleep in death on the battle-field are not forgotten by those highest in authority . . . .

The president would have a chance to speak to a widespread audience and remind them why the Civil War was being waged.

Lincoln also had less lofty reasons for going to Gettysburg. With the 1864 presidential election only a year away, here was an opportunity to rally important leaders of the Republican party. The governors of seventeen states were expected to attend this solemn occasion. Lincoln especially hoped to regain the support of Governor Curtin. The two men had had a falling out when Lincoln appointed Curtin's political rival Simon Cameron as his first secretary of war. The president's own bodyguard, Ward H. Lamon, was chief marshal of the ceremonies, in charge of security. A number of Lamon's friends were Pennsylvania politicians, with ties to the governor. So he was in a position to provide Lincoln with useful information.

The president's reelection could not be taken for granted because the political parties in the Northern states were split into feuding factions. Within the Democratic party were Copperheads, secretly supporting the South; Peace Democrats, eager for a negotiated settlement of the conflict and concerned about the loss of civil liberties; and War Democrats, wanting to go on fighting until the South was defeated. The Republican party was divided as well. Moderates accepted the way the war was being conducted and the measures taken to end slavery. Radicals, however, felt that Lincoln was too lenient toward the South, was not encouraging his commanders to fight the war hard enough, and was neglecting black civil rights. Pennsylvanian Thaddeus

the people for the people, shall not perish from the earth.

Stevens, an important Radical Republican leader in the House of Representatives, openly preferred Secretary of the Treasury Salmon P. Chase of Ohio as a presidential candidate. In his judgment, Lincoln was bound to lose. When Stevens heard that the president was going to Gettysburg, he commented, "Let the dead bury the dead." However, Lincoln was not to be so easily dismissed from the political arena.

While others questioned the odds of his political survival, Lincoln began to work on his speech. It may have been shaped by some interesting advice he had received earlier that fall. In September, before he was invited to Gettysburg, Lincoln had received a letter from railroad financier John M. Forbes, a Radical Republican, urging him to "teach your great audience of plain people that the war is not the North against the South, but the people against the aristocrats."

Forbes had spent the war in Boston mustering regiments of black troops. On November 3, Forbes's friend William Evans, a British politician, visited the president and encouraged him to become an international spokesman for democracy. Perhaps these suggestions may have helped set the tone and purpose of the president's remarks. Along similar lines, Lincoln undoubtedly recalled a statement he made during his debates in 1858 with Stephen Douglas:

"[T]here is no reason in the world why the negro is not entitled to all the natural rights enumerated in the Declaration of Independence, the right to life, liberty, and the pursuit of happiness."

By the Sunday before the dedication ceremonies, Lincoln commented to Noah Brooks, a close friend and journalist for the *Sacramento Daily Union*, that his speech was written "but not yet finished." He added that it was "short, short, short." He was

Washington, _____, 186 .

Four score and seven years ago our fathers brought

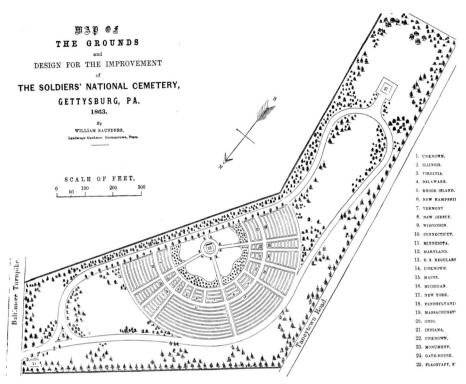

William Saunders's plan for the cemetery at Gettysburg

expected to say only a few well-chosen words, and they would be chosen with care.

As part of his preparation for the dedication ceremonies, the president invited William Saunders to the White House on November 17. The designer of the Gettysburg cemetery brought a copy of his plan for the gravesites with him. Saunders wrote that Lincoln "took much interest in it, asked about its surroundings, . . . and seemed familiar with the topography of the place although he had never been there."

forth, upon this continent, a new nation, conce

in liberty, and dedicated to the proposition th

According to Nicolay, by the time, Lincoln was ready to leave for Pennsylvania, he had completed the first nineteen lines of his address, ending with: "It is rather for us, the living, we here be dedica—." This first surviving draft of the speech was written in ink on Executive Mansion stationery without any corrections or insertions. Lincoln usually prepared his public statements quite carefully, spending many hours working and reworking his sentences and phrasings. So he probably wrote earlier versions of the speech, but these have never been found.

Executive Mansion,

Washington, _____, 186 .

Four score and seven years ago our fathers brought forth, upon this continent, a new nation, conceived in liberty, and dedicated to the proposition that "all men are created equal"

Now we are engaged in a great civil war, testing whether that nation, or any nation so conceived, and so dedicated, can long endure. We are met on a great battle field of that war. We have come to dedicate a portion of it, as a final resting place for those who died here, that the nation might live. This we may, in all propriety do. But, in a larger sense, we can not dedicate— we can not

The opening lines of Lincoln's first draft of the Gettysburg Address

Demands on his time kept him from completing the task. As commander in chief, Lincoln was responsible for overseeing the conduct of the war. In addition, he had to prepare his annual message to Congress, due in three weeks. He also greeted visitors to the White House, conducted cabinet meetings, and handled government business. On November 17, for example, he issued a proclamation fixing the starting point for the Union Pacific Railroad, as Congress required him to do.

Social events were also time-consuming. Earlier, on November 12, the president attended the wedding of Kate Chase, the daughter of his secretary of the treasury, to William Sprague, the governor of Rhode Island. Their reception was the highlight of the Washington social season. Lincoln's wife, Mary, did not accompany him since she was still in mourning for their middle son, Willie, who had died almost two years earlier at the age of eleven. In addition to his private sorrow over Willie's death, Lincoln now had new worries—his youngest son and "best chum," ten-year-old Tad, was bedridden with a fever, and doctors could not figure out what was wrong with him.

On November 17, Lincoln ordered his secretary of war, Edwin M. Stanton, to arrange a special train for the 80-mile (129-km) trip. On November 18, the president left for Gettysburg, without having finished his speech. According to historian Garry Wills, Stanton scheduled the departure for 6:00 A.M. on the day of the dedication, but Lincoln felt that they would need extra time and insisted that they leave the day before. He knew that the six-hour train ride could be subject to countless delays because of the wartime movement of troops and munitions on short notice. The four-car train, decorated with American flags and draped with patriotic bunting, drew crowds at every stop along the way.

*whether that nation, or any nation so concei
and so dedicated, can long endure. We are m*

Mary Todd Lincoln in 1861

Thomas "Tad" Lincoln

William "Willie" Lincoln

n a great battle field of that war. We have
ome to dedicate a portion of it, as a final rest-

The president greeted the spectators, accepting flowers and hugging babies, while more passengers joined the train.

Accompanying him on the trip were three members of the cabinet: Secretary of State William Seward, Secretary of the Interior John P. Usher, and Postmaster-General Montgomery Blair. The other heads of government departments had chosen to remain in Washington. Lincoln also brought with him diplomats from France and Italy, some politicians, his aides, Hay and Nicolay, Captain H. A. Wise, U.S. Navy, and Mrs. Wise (the daughter of Edward Everett), newspaper reporters, and a military honor guard.

John Hay

John Nicolay

ing place for those who died here, that the nation might live. This we may, in all propriety do. But, in

The last car had a parlor where Lincoln sat and talked with his guests. The president put everyone at ease, telling many stories, some sad, some humorous. When an elderly man boarded the train in Baltimore, he was introduced to Lincoln. The president consoled him after learning that he had lost his son at Gettysburg. Lincoln also managed to have discussions with visiting politicians, including Wayne MacVeagh, chairman of the Pennsylvania Republican party Central Committee.

The president excused himself from his guests as the train neared Gettysburg, explaining, "Gentlemen, this is all very pleasant, but the people will expect me to say something to them tomorrow, and I must give the matter some thought." This statement supports the claims made by reporter and editor Benjamin P. Poore and others that Lincoln wrote the Gettysburg Address "in the car on his way from Washington to the battlefield, upon a piece of pasteboard held on his knee." While their claim is certainly appealing and is offered as further proof of Lincoln's greatness, it is wrong. The president did not dash off the Gettysburg Address at the last minute and had already written a major portion of his speech in Washington. Possibly, he decided to polish and revise his speech during the train ride.

In the late afternoon, President Lincoln arrived in Gettysburg. He was greeted by Wills and Everett and escorted to Wills's home, two blocks away. His black servant William Slade took charge of the president's luggage and unpacked his clothing in a second-floor bedroom. Unlike Wills's other guests, Lincoln would not have to share his quarters. Those members of the presidential party who could not be accommodated in Wills's overcrowded home were given other lodgings in town. While a number of important officials dined with the president, Governor Curtin

larger sense, we can not dedicate— we can not consecrate— we can not hallow, this ground—

David Wills's house in Gettysburg

*The brave men, living and dead, who struggle
her, have hallowed it, far above our poor pow*

and his guests, including six other governors, arrived after the meal was served. Their train had been delayed, and it took them six hours to travel the 30 miles (48 km) between Harrisburg, the state capital, and Gettysburg. The president greeted the governor and spoke with Everett. During the evening, Everett probably gave Lincoln a copy of his speech so that the president could adjust his own remarks to avoid accidentally repeating or contradicting what the orator intended to say.

Throughout the town, roving military bands and glee clubs entertained in the streets, attracting many spectators. On this moonlit night, a crowd assembled at the Wills house and demanded that the president speak to them. Lincoln did not like to ad lib. He told them:

> *I appear before you, fellow-citizens, merely to thank you for this compliment. The inference is a very fair one that you hear me for a little while at least, were I to commence to make a speech. I do not appear before you for the purpose of doing so, and for several substantial reasons. The most substantial of these is that I have no speech to make. In my position it is somewhat important that I should not say foolish things. [A voice: "If you can help it."] It very often happens that the only way to help it is to say nothing at all. Believing that is my present condition this evening, I must beg of you to excuse me from addressing you further.*

The disappointed crowd then left to visit other distinguished officials, including Secretary Seward, who delivered a short speech to

add or detract. The world will little note, nor long remember what we say here; while it can never

Secretary of State William Henry Seward

them. Pennsylvanians Wayne MacVeagh and John W. Forney also spoke to them. Forney, a War Democrat, was a politician and editor whose Washington-based newspaper supported and defended the Lincoln administration. The two men spent much

Four score and seven years ago our fathers brought forth, upon this continent, a new nation, conceived in Liberty, and dedicated to the proposition that all men are created equal.

Now we are engaged in a great civil war, testing whether that nation, or any nation, so conceived, and so dedicated, can long endure. We are met here on a great battle-field of that war. We have come to dedicate a portion of it as a final resting place for those who here gave their lives that that nation might live. It is altogether fitting and proper that we should do this.

But in a larger sense we can not dedicate— we can not consecrate— we can not hallow this ground. The brave men, living and dead, who struggled here, have consecrated it far above our poor power to add or detract. The world will little note, nor long remember, what we say here, but

Lincoln's second draft of the Gettysburg Address

ted to the great task remaining before us—
that from these honored dead we take in-

of the evening eating and drinking with Hay and Nicolay, who were gathering political intelligence, trying to find out how local politicians felt about Lincoln.

Withdrawing to his bedroom around nine o'clock, the president sent his servant downstairs for some paper and pencils so he could work on his speech. Later, he walked across the street to the Harper's house where Secretary Seward was staying. They spent a half hour discussing recent telegrams from Washington. In addition to war bulletins, Secretary Stanton had wired the president: "On inquiry, Mrs. Lincoln informs me that your son is better this evening." In all likelihood, Lincoln brought his speech with him for Seward to read. After all, the secretary had looked at the president's First Inaugural Address and suggested ways to improve it.

The president went to bed around midnight and may have put the finishing touches to his speech the following morning, after breakfast. Wills and Pennsylvania Representative Edward MacPherson, one of his guests, claimed that the Gettysburg Address was written in Wills's house. What they failed to realize is that Lincoln had already written the first page of his speech in Washington. It is likely the president wrote or rewrote the conclusion in Gettysburg and made changes to the first page, neatly written in ink, with a lead pencil supplied by Wills. In view of the historic importance of the Gettysburg Address, it is not surprising that such different stories circulated about where and when it was written.

creased devotion to that cause for which they have given the last full measure of de-

CHAPTER FIVE

The Immediate Reaction to the Gettysburg Address

At Gettysburg, eyewitnesses disagreed about the impact of Lincoln's speech. In fact, a number of them recalled that it was not very successful. John R. Young, a reporter for the *Philadelphia Press*, disputed accounts published by Associated Press, *The New York Times*, and other newspapers. Their correspondents claimed that the speech had been interrupted at least five times by applause. Young was one of several observers who insisted that the audience applauded only briefly when the president concluded his remarks. There may have been an explanation for this, however. Editor and copublisher of the *Ohio State Journal*, Isaac Allen, reported:

> The President's calm but earnest utterances of this
> brief and beautiful address stirred the deepest foun-
> tains of feeling and emotion in the hearts of the
> vast throng before him, and when he had con-
> cluded, scarcely could an untearful eye be seen,

notion — that we here highly resolve these

dead shall not have died in vain, that

while sobs of smothered emotion were heard on every hand.

On the other hand, Allen's story is questionable. It was in his interest to provide a moving account of the speech. He was hoping that Lincoln would appoint him to a diplomatic post.

A more reasonable explanation of the audience's reaction is that they were tired and restless. On November 21, 1863, *The New York Times* reported that even while Everett spoke "there were as many people wandering about the fields . . . as stood around the stand listening to his eloquent periods." By the time Lincoln rose to speak, more than two hours later they would have been even more inattentive.

In his memoirs, Chief Marshal Ward Lamon also offered evidence that the Gettysburg Address was not well received. According to him, Everett and Seward discussed the speech just before Lincoln returned to his seat. The orator told the secretary of state, "It is not what I expected from him. I am disappointed." Seward agreed, commenting, "He had made a failure, and I am sorry for it. His speech was not equal to him." When they asked him for his opinion, Lamon stated, "I am sorry to say that it does not impress me as one of his great speeches."

According to Lamon, even Lincoln felt he had let his audience down. Right after he finished his speech, he told the marshal that he wished he had prepared it more carefully. Then he said, "Lamon, that speech won't *scour*! It is a flat failure, and the people are disappointed." Lincoln used the word scour frequently. It was a term farmers used for a plow that could not produce a straight furrow because the blade clogged with soil. For him, it meant an unworthy or unproductive activity.

the nation, shall have a new birth of freedom, and that government of the people by

Most historians dismiss Lamon's account as false and mis-leading. They consider his stories about his relationship with the president to be unreliable. Lamon was probably trying to impress people with his own importance. As Lincoln's bodyguard, he was close to the president, but there were other more reliable sources, who were even closer to the president. For example, presidential aide John Hay, another eyewitness, recorded in his diary that Lincoln spoke "in a firm free way, with more grace than is his wont." Later, in their biography of Lincoln, he and John Nicolay wrote that the speech was "eloquent, linking the deeds of the present to the thoughts of the future." They insisted that "the best critics have awarded it unquestioned rank as one of the world's masterpieces in rhetorical art."

Historians have even more important evidence that discredits Lamon's version of events. On November 20, the day after the dedication of the cemetery, Edward Everett praised the Gettysburg Address in a note he sent to President Lincoln:

> *Permit me also to express my great admiration of the thoughts expressed by you, with such eloquent simplicity and appropriateness, at the consecration of the cemetery. I should be glad if I could flatter myself that I came as near to the central idea of the occasion in two hours as you did in two minutes.*

Coming from him, this was high praise indeed. His written statement is much more believable than what Lamon claims to have overheard the famous orator say the previous day. Everett certainly did not have to compliment Lincoln's speech or compare it so favorably with his own.

The earliest known photographs of both Abraham Lincoln

Washington, _____, 186

Four score and seven years ago our fathers broug

and Mary Todd Lincoln, taken in 1842

...th, upon this continent, a new nation, conceived
...liberty, and dedicated to the proposition that

Lincoln's reply to Everett might seem to suggest that he was indeed disappointed with his own remarks. On the other hand, it is just as likely that Lincoln was being modest about his achievement. He was, after all, known as a humble man.

> *Your kind note of to-day is received. In our respective parts yesterday you could not have been excused to make a short address, nor I a long one. I am pleased to know that, in your judgment, the little I did say was not entirely a failure.*

In his note, he had made clear that Everett, not he, was the skilled orator invited to be the featured speaker at the dedication ceremony. Thus he was probably grateful for Everett's compliment.

If Lincoln truly had been ashamed of his speech or disappointed with the reaction to it, it is unlikely he would have wanted to preserve it. Yet he had made five handwritten copies of the Gettysburg Address. Hay and Nicolay each received early drafts of the speech. Scholars still argue over which of these copies was the one Lincoln used at Gettysburg. The issue has not been solved. Neither completely matches newspaper reporters' versions of the address. Also, each newspaper account is slightly different. Nevertheless, the Hay and Nicolay copies are regarded as the earliest versions of the speech. Both are preserved in the Library of Congress.

The president also sent copies to Wills and Everett. Wills wanted it for his official records of the dedication ceremonies. Everett intended to publish copies of all the Gettysburg speeches to raise money for a monument at the cemetery. His copy of the speech was auctioned off at the Metropolitan Fair in New York

"all men are created equal"

Now we are engaged in a great civil war, te...

City. Historian George Bancroft requested another copy to be lithographed and sold at the Soldiers and Sailors Fair in Baltimore. An unsuccessful speech could hardly have served as a fund-raiser. The handwritten sheets that Lincoln sent proved to be the wrong size to be duplicated. Colonel Alexander Bliss sent the president the right size paper. Lincoln recopied the speech. This version has been treated ever since as the official text of his speech.

Press coverage of the president's address was uneven. The big-city dailies focused on Everett's oration and treated Lincoln's speech as an afterthought. No headlines drew attention to the president's part in the dedication ceremonies. Overseas, the *London Times* largely ignored Lincoln's participation while reporting at length on Everett's performance. This is understandable. Everett had sent out advance copies of his speech to the newspapers, while Lincoln had not. Also, Everett, not Lincoln, was the main attraction.

On the other hand, many small weekly newspapers featured the president's address and reproduced it in its entirety. Their publishers did not have the space needed for complete coverage of Everett's oration. For them, Lincoln's 272-word speech was just the right length. As a result people in country towns across the United States were able to read and easily understand what the president said.

Editorial opinion about the Gettysburg Address divided along party lines. As might have been expected, editors of Democratic newspapers criticized the president and condemned his speech. The *Richmond Examiner*, voicing the opinions of Southern states, contained a particularly nasty attack on the events at Gettysburg. The editorial compared the dedication ceremonies to a "stage play," complete with "deep pathos" and "romantic drama," and "a vein of comedy." "On the present occasion Lincoln acted the clown." The *Chicago Times* commented, "It is not supposed by any one, we believe, that Mr. Lincoln is possessed of much polish in manners or conversation." The editorial argued that the president was "less refined than a savage."

In Harrisburg, Pennsylvania, a writer for the *Patriot and Union* dismissed Lincoln's speech as unimportant. It was described as an effort to strengthen the Republican party rather than to honor the dead. "We pass over the silly remarks of the President; for the credit of the nation we are willing that the veil of oblivion shall be dropped over them and that they shall no more be repeated or thought of." Other newspapers also accused the president of turning the dedication ceremony into a political campaign for his own and his party's reelection in 1864.

The correspondent for the *Chicago Times*, however, went further. He devoted part of his article to an analysis of the speech and found fault with it. According to him, Union soldiers did not die to "defend the proposition that all men are created equal"—as Lincoln had claimed—or any other abolitionist arguments against slavery. They died to uphold the Constitution and the Union. The article went on to reprint a number of clauses in the Constitution that allowed and protected slavery. The writer argued that as president, Lincoln had sworn to uphold the Constitution. Therefore he could not preach equality for slaves. For this reason, the article claimed, "the cheek of every American must tingle with shame as he reads the silly, flat, and dish-watery utterances of the man. . . . "

Editors and reporters for Republican newspapers treated the president's speech favorably and praised the way he gave it. For

on a great battle field of that war. We have come to dedicate a portion of it, as a final re

example, an article in the *Springfield Republican*, a Massachusetts paper, described the Gettysburg Address as "a perfect gem; deep in feeling, compact in thought and expression." The writer went on to note, apologetically:

> *We had grown so accustomed to homely and imperfect phrase in his productions that we had come to think it was the law of his utterance. But this shows that he can talk handsomely as well as act sensibly.*

Obviously, the members of the Gettysburg commission were not the only ones to question the president's oratorical skills and to object to his folksy style.

The *Springfield Republican* stated that Lincoln had given an even better speech than Edward Everett. This view was also echoed in the *Philadelphia Evening Bulletin*, the *Providence Journal*, and the *Detroit Advertiser and Tribune*. The correspondent for *Harper's Weekly* made a similar comparison: "The oration by Mr. Everett was smooth and cold. . . . The few words by the President were from the heart to the heart. They can not be read, even, without kindling emotion." He included a quotation from Lincoln's speech as an example of the president's sincerity and depth of feeling. "The world will little note nor long remember what we say here, but it can never forget what they did here." Lincoln might have been surprised to learn that future generations of Americans would remember what he said at Gettysburg.

⌒ CHAPTER SIX ⌒
An Immortal Speech

Why did the president's words inspire Americans? First, his style appealed to them. Lincoln's speech was more modern than Everett's oration. Instead of using flowery, complicated phrases, the president expressed his ideas in a simpler, briefer form. According to historian Garry Wills, Lincoln was already familiar with the rhythm and speed of the telegraph, a recent invention in his day. In his speeches and his dispatches to his generals, Lincoln deliberately chose simple words so that his messages would be readily transmitted over the wire and clearly understood. He used the language people actually spoke rather than the stately terms and phrases of literary classics that Everett used. No wonder that people could grasp the president's ideas with little effort.

Second, what Lincoln had to say at Gettysburg was moving. He appealed to people's emotions as well as their intellect. Unlike Everett, he did not recount the details of the Battle of Gettysburg, nor did he analyze the specific causes of the War Between the States. Instead, he gave a talk about ideals. He spoke in general

larger sense, we can not dedicate—we can no consecrate—we can not hallow, this ground—

terms, which are still meaningful to people today. The president drew upon the Christian creed of sacrifice, death, and rebirth to help people make sense of the grisly scenes they had witnessed. He stated that costly, terrible, bloody battles like Gettysburg were fought to give Americans a new chance to live up to their ideals, to live in freedom under a democratic government. The message was simple, but the reasoning that Lincoln used was complex.

Like American statesmen Daniel Webster and Henry Clay, Lincoln regarded the Declaration of Independence of 1776, rather than the Constitution of 1787, as the foundation of American beliefs. In his Gettysburg Address, his reference to "four score and seven years ago" (1776) implied that the American people had bonded together as a nation before the Constitution was written, in 1787. The president was suggesting that the nation was founded when the people of the colonies announced their separation from Great Britain. The states did not create the federal government; the people did. Furthermore, the Articles of Confederation and the Constitution were attempts to form "a more perfect Union," not to first form a union.

From this point of view, Lincoln could never regard the United States as a mere compact among independent states, which could be broken, a view popular in the South. He saw the Civil War as a "domestic insurrection," a family quarrel, not a conflict between two separate nations, as the South claimed. Union armies were fighting to restore order and normal relationships, not to conquer territories and peoples.

The Declaration claimed that officials received their powers from the "consent of the governed." The War Between the States struck at this basic principle by challenging majority rule. In 1861, when the conflict started, Lincoln insisted:

We must settle this question now, whether in a free
government the minority have the right to break up
the government whenever they choose. If we fail, it
will go far to prove the incapability of the people to
govern themselves.

At Gettysburg, the president urged Americans to make sure "that government of the people, by the people, and for the people shall not perish from the earth." For him, the Civil War was being fought to prove that democracy could work, that people could indeed govern themselves. In his first message to Congress, in 1861, Lincoln had described the war as "a People's contest," a contest to maintain a government whose purpose was to "elevate the condition of men" to give everyone a "fair chance, in the race of life."

Another important ideal set forth in the Declaration can be found in the statement, "We hold these truths to be self-evident, that all Men are created equal." Thus at Gettysburg, Lincoln could claim that the nation was "dedicated to the proposition that all men are created equal." The Constitution, however, made no such claim. It had even legalized slavery.

Slavery was a denial of the principles of the Declaration of Independence. Lincoln clearly saw it as an evil, but as president, he had sworn to uphold the Constitution. In a letter written in 1864, he stated:

I am naturally anti-slavery. If slavery is not
wrong, nothing is wrong. I can not remember when
I did not so think, and feel. And yet I have never

> *understood that the Presidency conferred upon me*
> *an unrestricted right to act officially upon this*
> *judgment and feeling.*

He knew that under the Constitution, neither he nor Congress had the power to free slaves. Such a change required a constitutional amendment.

The president had issued the Emancipation Proclamation of 1862. It only freed slaves in the Southern states that rebelled against the Union. He took this action as commander in chief of the nation's armed forces. He was acting within his powers under the Constitution. Lincoln defended his decision as a military necessity, to deprive the South of its property and warmaking ability. In 1862 he wrote in a letter:

> *My paramount object in this struggle is to save the*
> *Union . . . . If I could save the Union without*
> *freeing any slave I would do it, and if I could save*
> *it by freeing some and leaving others alone I would*
> *also do that.*

His decision disappointed the abolitionists, who viewed the war as a crusade against slavery. He disagreed with many of their views. Back in 1858, Lincoln had denied that whites and blacks could ever be social or political equals. At best he wanted them to have economic freedom, "the right to eat bread without leave of anybody else, which his own hand earns. . . ." His solution to race relations was to encourage blacks to colonize other lands, like Liberia, a position also held by Thomas Jefferson and Henry Clay.

forget what they did here.
It is rather for us, the living, we here be dedicated to stand here,

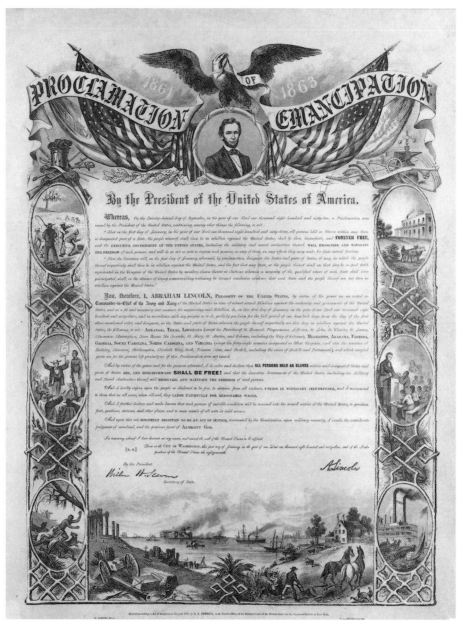

A print of the Emancipation Proclamation

ted to the great task remaining before us—

that from these honored dead we take in-

Lincoln did not rely on the moral arguments of the aboli-tionists when he freed the slaves. He did not want to further antagonize the South. He expected that after the war he would be president of the South as well as the North. He also knew that many people in the Northern states would not give their lives for this cause. They would fight, however, to restore the Union. In sum, while he did feel that slavery was morally wrong, legal, prac-tical, and political issues kept him from freeing all the slaves—from applying the ideals of the Declaration of Independence in violation of the Constitution.

Lincoln used the Declaration to offer the American people a promising vision of the future. It stated that they were entitled to "certain unalienable Rights, that among these are Life, Liberty, and the Pursuit of Happiness." Faced with so many battlefield deaths, Lincoln encouraged Americans to renew their faith in the ideals of the Declaration and to extend them to future genera-tions. This was what Lincoln called a "new birth of freedom" in his Gettysburg speech. He wanted them to practice what the Declaration of Independence preached.

Overall, the Gettysburg Address presented Lincoln's eloquent explanation of the reasons the Civil War was fought. More impor-tant, it restated basic American ideals. Of course, a few historians claimed that the speech was merely a masterful piece of wartime propaganda. Others even dismissed it as an attempt to rally sup-port for the Republican party in the upcoming elections.

Such claims lost much of their significance on April 14, 1865. On that day a Southerner, John Wilkes Booth, shot and killed Abraham Lincoln. He was the first president to be assassinated. Because Lincoln rose from humble beginnings, the people felt they had lost one of their own, a commoner, just like them.

creased. devotion to that cause for which
they have, gave the last free measure of ou-

Despite his rise to power, he had never lost touch with ordinary citizens. In their grief, the American people turned to Lincoln's legacy of speeches and sought comfort in his words. To many, his death was a sacrifice for the Union and for democracy, like the fallen at Gettysburg. His assassination ensured that they would never forget what he said at Gettysburg two years earlier.

In the twentieth century, Lincoln's speech inspired writers, composers, filmmakers, and other presidents. For example, poet Robert Lowell commented, "By his words he gave the battlefield a significance that it had lacked. . . . I believe this is a meaning that goes beyond sect or religion and beyond peace and war, and is now part of our lives as a challenge, obstacle, and hope." Composer Aaron Copland's magnificent *Lincoln Portrait* (1942) concludes with a narrator reciting the last lines of the Gettysburg Address. The speech was also featured in *Ruggles of Red Gap*, a 1935 movie about a proper British servant in the Wild West. Wanting to prove how American he had become, the Englishman recited the address to group of cowboys in a saloon and won their respect.

One of many presidents to pay tribute to Lincoln, Democratic President Franklin D. Roosevelt spoke at Gettysburg in 1938, noting:

> *For the issue which he restated on this spot seventy-five years ago, . . . will be the continuing issue before this nation so long as we cling to the purposes for which it was founded—to preserve under the changing conditions of each generation, a people's government for a people's good.*

notion—that we here highly resolve these dead shall not have died in vain; that

The New-York Times.

…IV......NO. 4230. NEW-YORK, SATURDAY, APRIL 15, 1865. PRICE FOUR CENT

…L EVENT.

…nt Lincoln …t by an …ssassin.

…Done at Ford's …e Last Night.

A DESPERATE REBEL

…ent Still Alive at …t Accounts.

…Entertained of His …ecovery.

…Assassination of …ary Seward.

…E DREADFUL TRAGEDY.

[OFFICIAL.]
WAR DEPARTMENT, …INGTON, April 15—1 30 A. M.

…t about 9.30 P. M., at Ford's …sident, while sitting in his … Mrs. LINCOLN, Mrs. HARRIS, …OURN, was shot by an assas… …y entered the box and ap… the President.

…en leaped upon the stage, …ge dagger or knife, and made … rear of the theatre.

…entered the back of the Pre… … penetrated nearly through …wound is mortal. The Presi… …ensible ever since it was in… …w dying.

… hour an assassin, whether …entered Mr. SEWARD's apart… … the pretence of having a … shown to the Secretary's … The assassin immediately …, and inflicted two or three

…box, waving a long dagger in his right hand, and exclaiming "*Sic semper tyrannis,*" and immediately leaped from the box, which was in the second tier, to the stage beneath and ran across to the opposite side, making his escape amid the bewilderment of the audience from the rear of the theatre, and mounting a horse, fled.

The screams of Mrs. LINCOLN first disclosed the fact to the audience that the President had been shot, when all present rose to their feet, rushing toward the stage, many exclaiming "Hang him! hang him!"

The excitement was of the wildest possible description, and of course there was an abrupt termination of the theatrical performance.

There was a rush toward the President's box, when cries were heard: "Stand back and give him air." "Has any one stimulants." On a hasty examination, it was found that the President had been shot through the head, above and back of the temporal bone, and that some of the brain was oozing out. He was removed to a private house opposite to the theatre, and the Surgeon-General of the army, and other surgeons sent for to attend to his condition.

On an examination of the private box blood was discovered on the back of the cushioned rocking chair on which the President had been sitting, also on the partition and on the floor. A common single-barreled pocket pistol was found on the carpet.

A military guard was placed in front of the private residence to which the President had been conveyed. An immense crowd was in front of it, all deeply anxious to learn the condition of the President. It had been previously announced that the wound was mortal, but all hoped otherwise. The shock to the community was terrible.

The President was in a state of syncope, totally insensible, and breathing slowly. The blood oozed from the wound at the back of his head. The surgeons exhausted every effort of medical skill, but all hope was gone. The parting of his family with the dying President is too sad for description.

At midnight, the Cabinet, with Messrs. SUMNER, COLFAX and FARNSWORTH, Judge CURTIS, Gov. OGLESBY, Gen. MEIGS, Col. HAY, and a few personal friends, with Surgeon-General BARNES and his immediate assistants, were around his bedside.

The President and Mrs. LINCOLN did not start for the theatre until fifteen minutes after

…Department and two male nurses, disabling them all, he then rushed upon the Secretary, who was lying in bed in the same room, and inflicted three stabs in the neck, but severing, it is thought and hoped, no arteries, though he bled profusely.

The assassin then rushed down stairs, mounted his horse at the door, and rode off before an alarm could be sounded, and in the same manner as the assassin of the President.

It is believed that the injuries of the Secretary are not fatal, nor those of either of the others, although both the Secretary and the Assistant Secretary are very seriously injured.

Secretaries STANTON and WELLES, and other prominent officers of the government, called at Secretary SEWARD's house to inquire into his condition, and there heard of the assassination of the President.

They then proceeded to the house where he was lying, exhibiting of course intense anxiety and solicitude. An immense crowd was gathered in front of the President's house, and a strong guard was also stationed there, many persons evidently supposing he would be brought to his home.

The entire city to-night presents a scene of wild excitement, accompanied by violent expressions of indignation, and the profoundest sorrow—many shed tears. The military authorities have dispatched mounted patrols in every direction, in order, if possible, to arrest the assassins. The whole metropolitan police are likewise vigilant for the same purpose.

The attacks, both at the theatre and at Secretary SEWARD's house, took place at about the same hour—10 o'clock—thus showing a preconcerted plan to assassinate those gentlemen. Some evidence of the guilt of the party who attacked the President are in the possession of the police.

Vice-President JOHNSON is in the city, and his headquarters are guarded by troops.

ANOTHER ACCOUNT.

Special Dispatch to the New-York Times.

WASHINGTON, Friday, April 14, 11.15 P. M.

A stroke from Heaven laying the whole of the city in instant ruins could not have startled us as did the word that broke from Ford's Theatre a half hour ago that the President had been shot. It flew everywhere

though every body supposes them to have been rebels.

SATURDAY MORNING –1 O'CLOCK.

The person who shot the President is represented as about 30 years of age, five feet nine inches in height, sparely built, of light complexion, dressed in dark clothing, and having a genteel appearance. He entered the box, which is known as the State box, being the upper box on the right hand side from the dress-circle in the regular manner, and shot the President from behind, the ball entering the skull about in the middle, behind, and going in the direction of the left eye; it did not pass through, but apparently broke the frontal bone and forced out the brain to some extent. The President is not yet dead, but is wholly insensible, and the Surgeon-General says he cannot live till day-break. The assassin was followed across the stage by a gentleman, who sprang out from an orchestra chair. He rushed through the side door into an alley, thence to the avenue and mounted a dark bay horse, which he apparently received from the hand of an accomplice, dashed up F, toward the back part of the city. The escape was so sudden that he effectually eluded pursuit. The assassin cried "*sic sempre*" in a sharp, clear voice, as he jumped to the stage, and dropped his hat and a glove.

Two or three officers were in the box with the President and Mrs. LINCOLN, who made efforts to stop the assassin, but were unsuccessful, and received some bruises. The whole affair, from his entrance into the box to his escape from the theatre, occupied scarcely a minute, and the strongest of the action found everybody wholly unprepared. The assault upon Mr. SEWARD appeares to have been made almost at the same moment as that upon the President. Mr. SEWARD's wound is not dangerous in itself, but may prove so in connection with his recent injuries. The two assassins have both endeavored to leave the city to the northwest, apparently not expecting to strike the river. Even so low down as Chain Bridge, cavalry have been sent in every direction to intercept them.

SATURDAY, 1 30 o'clock A. M.

The President still lies insensible. Messrs. STANTON, WELLS, McCULLOCH, SPEED and USHER are with him, as also the Vice-President, the Surgeon-General, and other Surgeons.

There is a great throng about the house, even at this hour.

EUROPEAN NEWS.

TWO DAYS LATER BY THE EUROPA.

The Insult to Our Cruisers by Portugal.

The American Minister at Lisbon Demands Satisfaction.

Dismissal of the Commander of Fort Belan Requested.

Further Advance in Five-Twenties.

FINANCIAL AND COMMERCIAL.

HALIFAX, Friday, April 14.

The steamship *Europa*, from Liverpool on the 1st, via Queenstown on the 2d inst., arrived here at 2 o'clock this morning. She has 43 passengers for this port, and 30 for Boston. Her dates are two days later than those already received.

The steamship *Cuba*, from New-York, arrived at Liverpool at noon on the 1st inst.

THE STONEWALL AFFAIR.

A Lisbon dispatch, of the 31st of March, says that the American Minister at Lisbon has demanded satisfaction of the Portuguese Government for the firing upon the *Niagara* and *Sacremento* by the Portuguese forts. He also requests the dismissal of the Commander of Fort Belan, and a salute of twenty-one guns to the American flag.

Nothing as yet has been decided in regard to the matter.

A PROPHECY FROM RICHMOND.

The correspondent of the London *Times*, writing from Richmond on the 4th of March, says:

"I am daily more convinced that if Richmond falls and LEE and JOHNSTON are driven from the field, it is but the first stage of this colossal revolution which will then be completed. There will ensue a time when every important town of the South will require to be held by a Yankee garrison, when exultation in New-York will be exchanged for soberness and right reason, and when it will be realized that the closing scenes of this mightiest revolutionary drama will not be played out, save in the times of our children's children."

GREAT BRITAIN.

Parliamentary proceedings on the 30th ult. were unimportant.

In the House of Commons, on the 31st, Lord C. PAGET said that the Admiralty had received no proposal for sanctioning or supporting any fresh attempt to reach the North Pole. He was, therefore, unable to say what course the government would take if such a proposal were made.

Mr. NEWDEGATE put some questions as to the idea of the Pope taking up his residence in England, as indicated in some foreign journals.

Lord PALMERSTON replied that the government respected the Pope personally very much, but for him to come to England would be both an anachronism and a solecism.

The revenue returns for the financial year, ending March 31, show a net increase of over £104,000 on the year. Notwithstanding the great reductions in taxation, the revenue exceeds by nearly half a million sterling the estimates of Mr. GLADSTONE.

Messrs. BARING's circular says that large business has been done in 5-20 bonds, and that prices advanced early in the week to 57¼@58, but have since relapsed to 56½@57—the demand being chiefly from the continent.

…omire, but must maintain the position of Aus… a great Power.

INDIA.

A private Calcutta telegram of March … ports commercial affairs in much the same … on the 25th, when slight improvement had taken…

BRAZIL.

LONDON, Sunday, A…

The Brazilian mail has reached Lisbon, …ing the following dates:

RIO DE JANEIRO, Saturday, Mar…
Exchange 25¾@26¼.
COFFEE.—Sales of good firsts at 8$100. Shi… 100,000 bags. Stock, 100 000 bags. Freights …
BAHIA, Saturday, Mar…
Exchange 26¼.
Cotton nominal.
PERNAMBUCO, Saturday, Mar…
Exchange 26¾@27.
Montevedeo has surrendered to Gen. FLORES… Brazilians now occupy the city.

LATEST VIA LIVERPOOL.

LIVERPOOL, Saturday Evening, April 1…

The *Times* to-day has an editorial … amended tariff law of the United States. … "It is impossible to find an excuse for it, … by the light of reason or by the results of exp… it is alike condemned."

It ironically credits the framers of the … with peculiar wisdom in selecting the 1st … for its inauguration.

The *Army & Navy Gazette* says: "The … the United States Navy has now been accom… and it must be confessed that in the hands … …AGUT and PORTER the high reputation wh… officers and seamen of that Power establish… after the national existence of itself, has been … enhanced."

LATEST VIA QUEENSTOWN.

LONDON, Saturday, A…

There is no news of importance this m…

PARIS, Friday, March 31–…

The Bourse is steady. The Rentes cl… 67f. 30c.

COMMERCIAL.

LIVERPOOL MARKET.

LIVERPOOL, April 31.—E…

The Market report was received per *Moravian*… COTTON—The stock of Cotton in port is 540 000 … actual count, being 13,000 bales below the est… which amount 45,000 bales are American.

TRADE REPORT.

The Manchester market was firmer with a… tendency.

BREADSTUFFS—The market is easier. Messrs. … …SON, SPENCE & Co., and others, report Flour … easier. Wheat quiet and quotations are barely … ed; red Western 8s.@8s. 6d. Corn inactive … 27s. 6d.

PROVISIONS—The market is downward. W… NASH & Co., and others, report: Beef has a d… tendency. Pork heavy and declined 2s. 6d… firmer and holders demand an advance. Lard … easier at 5…@…s. Butter flat and declining … downward.

PRODUCE.—Ashes easier at 2…s. 6d. for Pots… for Pearls. Sugar, flat. Coffee, quiet and stea… quiet and steady. Clover Seed, firmer. Jute, … lower. Cod Oil, quiet at 57s. Sperm Oil, no sa… seed Oil, steady. Resin, very dull. Spirits Tu… quiet at 65s.@…s.

PETROLEUM—HOULT, EVOLINE & BRANDON re… troleum firm, at 1s. 11d.@2s. for refined; no … market.

LONDON MARKETS.

FLOUR firm; WHEAT steady. IRON advanc… and rails, £6 10s.@£6 15s.; Scotch pig, 52s. 3d… inactive. COFFEE active at a decline of 1s. … steady at 10¾d. for common Congou. RIC… SPIRITS TURPENTINE firm at 47s. PETROLEUM … £18 for crude, 2s. for refined. SPERM OIL nomin… TALLOW downward, at 40s.@43s. LINSEED OIL…

LATEST COMMERCIAL.

LIVERPOOL, Saturday, April 1—E…

COTTON—Sales to-day 6,000 bales, including … to speculators and exporters. The market is … but quiet and unchanged.

BREADSTUFFS—The market is quiet and stead…

PROVISIONS—The market is dull.

PRODUCE—The market is quiet and steady… leum firm at 2s.@2s. 6½d for refined.

LONDON, Saturday, April 1—E…

CONSOLS closed at 89⅞@90 for money.

AMERICAN STOCKS—Illinois Central Railro… 62¼; Erie Railroad 36¼@36¾; United Sta… twenties 57⅝@58¼.

Gen. Lee in Richmond—The Oath …

The New York Times, front page, Saturday, April 15, 1865

the nation, shall have a new birth of freedom, and that government of the people by

Lincoln's funeral procession through New York City

the people for the people, shall not perish from the earth.

Lincoln may have wanted all Americans to enjoy the "unalienable rights" promised by the Declaration of Independence. Yet this did not happen for many years. A series of false starts and broken promises were made from 1865 to 1870 in the Thirteenth, Fourteenth, and Fifteenth Amendments to the Constitution. It wasn't until the mid-twentieth century that blacks were finally able to fully participate in American life. While the Nineteenth Amendment gave women the right to vote in 1920, they also struggled through the remainder of the century to achieve equality with men. With the passage of time, Americans have redefined equality not only to include the right to take part in politics but also to have the opportunity to compete for success without regard to race, religion, gender, or national origin. Recent demands have included equal pay for equal work and the right to join social and fraternal groups without prejudice.

Definitions of liberty have also changed over time as well as relations between the rulers and the ruled. Lincoln was identified with powerful leadership as well as democracy. Until the 1930s, however, people feared that a strong government would take away their freedom. They did not want officials to interfere in their lives. Then with the collapse of the national economy in the 1930s, the public began to welcome government programs to put them back to work, to reform businesses and working conditions, and to give them money to buy food and other necessities of life.

In the 1980s, people shifted somewhat to the older view of government. They demanded that lawmakers cut government programs and regulations. They wanted to make their own decisions, to take charge of their own lives again. They resented government rules telling them how to run their businesses and whom they could employ, giving handouts to the needy, or ban-

Washington, _____, 186 .

Four score and seven years ago our fathers brought

The Lincoln Memorial in Washington, D.C.

forth, upon this continent, a new nation, conce
in liberty, and dedicated to the proposition th

ning religious observances in schools. As a result, welfare programs were cut back, and controls over such industries as trucking, banking, the airlines, and telephones were lifted.

Lincoln's promise of a "new birth of freedom" and a "government of the people, by the people, and for the people" are still important goals. In the twenty-first century, advances in computer technology and rapid communication may make it possible for Americans to make his vision a reality. Technology will enable more people to voice their opinions and to actually take part in government decisions affecting their lives. However, with new technology will probably come new challenges to freedom and equality. This is why every generation will continue to turn to Lincoln's Gettysburg Address for inspiration.

The first two of Lincoln's handwritten copies of the Gettysburg Address can be found in the Library of Congress. His speech is engraved alongside a bust of the president at the Gettysburg cemetery, a national park since 1895. His famous words are also inscribed on a wall of the Lincoln Memorial in Washington D.C., dedicated in May 1922. They can be found on monuments to the slain president in many of the states. What the president said at Gettysburg on November 19, 1863, has become immortal. It will continue to remind Americans to live up to the ideals of the nation's founders.

"all men are created equal"

⤳ *Sources* ⤳

Brooks, Noah. *Washington, D.C. in Lincoln's Time*, ed. Herbert Mitgang. Chicago: Quadrangle Books, 1971.

Burlingame, Michael and John R. Turner Ettlinger, eds. *Inside Lincoln's White House: The Complete Civil War Diary of John Hay.* Carbondale: Southern Illinois University Press, 1997.

Burrage, Henry Sweetser. *Gettysburg and Lincoln.* New York: G.P. Putnam's Sons, 1906.

Everett, Edward. *Orations and Speeches on Various Occasions.* 4 vols. Boston: Little, Brown and Company, 1868, vol. 4, pp. 623–659.

Harper, Robert S. *Lincoln and the Press.* New York: McGraw-Hill Book Company, Inc., 1951.

Lamon, Ward Hill. *Recollections of Abraham Lincoln, 1847–1865.* Lincoln: University of Nebraska Press, (1895) 1994.

Leckie, Robert. *None Died in Vain.* New York: HarperCollins, 1990.

Lincoln as They Saw Him, ed. Herbert Mitgang. New York: Rinehart & Company, Inc., 1956.

McPherson, James P. *Abraham Lincoln and the Second American Revolution.* New York: Oxford University Press, 1991.

———. ed. *We Cannot Escape History: Lincoln and the Last Best Hope of Earth.* Urbana: University of Illinois Press, 1995.

Nicolay, John G. and John Hay. *Abraham Lincoln: A History.* 10 vols. New York: The Century Company, 1890, vol. 1.

Peterson, Merrill D. *Lincoln in American Memory.* New York: Oxford University Press, 1994.

Reminiscences of Abraham Lincoln by Distinguished Men of His Time, ed. Allen Thorndike Rice. New York: Haskell House Publishers, (1888) 1971.

Sandberg, Carl. *Abraham Lincoln: The War Years.* 4 vols. New York: Harcourt Brace and Company, 1939, vol. 2, pp. 452–477.

Thayer, William Roscoe. *John Hay.* 2 vols. New York: Kraus Reprint Company, (1908) 1969, vol. 1.

Wills, Garry. *Lincoln at Gettysburg.* New York: Simon & Schuster, 1992.

Young, John Russell. "Lincoln Delivers the Gettysburg Address," *Eyewitness to America.* ed. David Colbert. New York: Vintage Books, 1998, pp. 263–267.

WEB SITES:

Library of Congress Home Page lcweb@loc.gov

Lincoln's Collected Works http://www.alinconassoc.com

⮂ Further Reading ⮀

Beller, Susan P. *To Hold This Ground: A Desperate Battle at Gettysburg*. New York: Simon & Schuster, 1995.

Bial, Raymond. *Where Lincoln Walked*. New York: Walker & Company, 1998.

Freedman, Russell. *Lincoln: A Photobiography*. New York: Clarion, 1987.

Lindop, Edmund. *James K. Polk, Abraham Lincoln, Theodore Roosevelt* (*Presidents Who Dared* series). Brookfield, CT: Twenty-First Century Books, 1995.

Murphy, Jim. *The Long Road to Gettysburg*. New York: Clarion, 1992.

Sandburg, Carl. *Abe Lincoln Grows Up*. San Diego: Harcourt Brace, 1975.

There are many Web sites featuring Abraham Lincoln and the Gettysburg Address. Web sites expire and change, so in addition to the following, you may also want to search the Internet for further information.

http://www.loc.gov/exhibits/gadd/gadrft.html
This Library of Congress Web site features the John Hay and John Nicolay versions of Gettysburg Address. The site also gives the locations of the three further copies Lincoln wrote himself.

http://www.thelincolnmuseum.org/main.html
Web site of the Lincoln Museum featuring history and quizzes

http://www.nps.gov/liho/
This National Parks Web site of the Lincoln home has a wide range of information, including some of Lincoln's autobiographical writings.

⚘ Index ⚘

ᘒ About the Author ᘒ

Barbara Silberdick Feinberg graduated with honors from Wellesley College where she was elected to Phi Beta Kappa. She holds a Ph.D. in political science from Yale University.

Among her more recent works are *Watergate: Scandal in the White House*; *American Political Scandals Past and Present*; *The National Government, State Governments, Local Governments*; *Words in the News: A Student's Dictionary of American Government and Politics*; *Harry S. Truman*; *John Marshall: The Great Chief Justice*; *Electing the President*; *The Cabinet*; *Hiroshima and Nagasaki*; *Black Tuesday: The Stock Market Crash of 1929*; *Term Limits for Congress*; *The Constitutional Amendments*; *Next in Line: The American Vice Presidency*; *Patricia Ryan Nixon*; *Elizabeth Wallace Truman*; *Edith Kermit Carow Roosevelt*; *America's First Ladies: Changing Expectations*; *General Douglas MacArthur: An American Hero*; and *The Dictionary of the U.S. Constitution*. She has also written *Marx and Marxism*; *The Constitution: Yesterday, Today, and Tomorrow*; and *Franklin Roosevelt, Gallant President* and contributed entries to *The Young Reader's Companion to American History*.

Mrs. Feinberg lives in New York City with her Yorkshire terrier Holly. Among her hobbies are growing African violets, collecting autographs of historic personalities, listening to the popular music of the 1920s, 30s, and 40s, and working out in exercise classes.